Books by Dennis M Keating

The Olympics:
An Unauthorized Unsanctioned History
*
Charlie Whitman
Was a Friend of Mine
*
Ena Road
*
The Fulda Gap
*
A Chicago Tale
*
Black Lahu
*
Poetry for Men

2

BLACK LAHU

LIFE AND DEATH
IN THE TRIANGLE

Dennis M Keating

This book was created by
the Golden Sphere team
in coordination with the Honolulu Guy,
Dennis M Keating

www.goldensphere.com

The Author

Dennis M Keating

The Honolulu Guy

DEDICATION

To the Hill Tribes
of
Southeast Asia

ACKNOWLEDMENTS

Thanks to

Professor Steven Taylor Goldsberry
My Mentor

Paula Marie Fernandez and Hikari Kimura
For Artwork and Maps

Gail M Baugniet and Faith Scheideman
Advisors and Proofreaders

Sandy
My Wife, Proponent and Ally

BLACK LAHU

Life and Death
in the Triangle

*

A Narrative Poem
written in
Rhyming Couplets

BY

DENNIS M KEATING

The Black Lahu are one of several Hill Tribes that lived in the mountainous areas of Southeast Asia. Their traditional lifestyles do not easily fit in with our way of life, nor our modern concepts of country borders and big city life.

Dennis M Keating first traveled to Southeast Asia in the early 1970's. Since then, his life has intertwined with the area.

BLACK LAHU

In my youth,

I enjoyed adventurous tales,

Of jungle dangers

And smuggler trails.

Being fascinated

By intriguing scenes,

The Golden Triangle

Lit my radar screens.

So, it was, some

Six decades ago,

The Triangle's mysteries

I wanted to know.

THE GOLDEN TRIANGLE

I fixated on the Triangle
As a cool place to stray.

But then, life's realities
Got in the way.

School, family, job, and money,

All came first,

Before I could fulfill

My wanderlust thirst.

Gradually,
These issues got resolved.

Events unfolded.

My life evolved.

The Golden Triangle is the area in Southeast Asia that produces opium. The Black Lahu are one of the hill tribes living in the Golden Triangle.

In the Triangle, Burma, Thailand and Laos are the major opium trade players. China and the other neighboring countries play lesser roles.

While China is not normally viewed a as part of the Golden Triangle, my personal experiences in Chinese and Thai border towns motivates me to view China as a Triangle country. This said, Chinese history has been entwined with the opium business for hundreds of years; long before the Opium Wars of the 1800's. Also, the Chinese Diaspora to other Asian countries has often played a part in the opium trade. A Diaspora is the movement of a large group of people from their homeland to other countries.

Meanwhile, through books and maps

I'd glance,

Noting the four countries

In the Triangle's expanse.

Burma and Thailand

Are its main part.

They are the Triangle's

Soul and heart.

Laos and China round

Out the four.

These two shielded
Burma's back door.

The Gold in the Golden Triangle name relates to the income that is generated from the cultivated poppies. One reason concerns the fact that early Chinese traders used gold as their primary currency.

In general, the poor villagers in these remote areas have been subsistence farmers for centuries. They produced just enough food to maintain their small villages.

Long ago, the village farmers learned opium poppy seeds were the one item outside traders would eagerly buy from them. The extra money they earned afforded them opportunities to buy medicine and other things their local crops did not provide.

They play lesser roles,

It's true.

But they do provide

A protective glue.

I consider Burma

To be the Triangle's heart,

So, I chose Rangoon

As the place to start.

It took maybe a week,

Certainly, not more,

For me to learn I'd picked

The wrong door.

Rangoon Burma

Burma became an independent republic in 1948. Just like the Republic of Ireland three decades earlier, Burma chose to go it alone and break away from its former British overlords.

Since that time, Burma has had many honorable and well respected civilian leaders and many despicable and corrupt military leaders.

The local youths truly

Welcomed me.

All eager to learn of

The Land of the Free.

But when we talked

They kept a watchful eye.

Any passing stranger

Might be a Junta spy.

Big Brother cared,

I had no doubt.

Many eyes watched

Whenever I went out.

Burma – The former name of the country now known as Myanmar. Old timers who consider the military Junta despots to be illegal continue to call the country Burma.

Junta – A military group that takes power by force.

Rangoon – The main city and former capital of Burma.

US Marines – Since 1949, Marines have been deployed to US embassies around the world to protect our diplomats and classified information.

Old Corps – A former active duty Marine. Young Marines have deep respect for those Marines who went before them and served at a prior time in the Old Corps.

And my room was searched
Each time I left.

But my used rolls of film
Were the only theft.

Our embassy Marines befriended me.

I was Old Corps.

They chauffeured me round town,

And filled me in on the score.

All were Asian Americans,

Who our government chose.

When off duty, they blended well

In civilian clothes.

Asian Americans – At the more sensitive US embassies in Asia, our government tries to assign Asian American Marines. Often, they are called upon to drive embassy staff and their family to appointments or meetings. In these circumstances the Marines wear civilian clothes. As Asian Americans, they blend in and don't attract attention to themselves.

Laos - A communistic country that is tightly controlled by a military clique.

Vientiane - The capital city of Laos. It borders Thailand and is the major city of Laos.

Kickback – A bribe or payoff.

My pretty tour guide seemed eager

To be my special friend.

I felt a romantic relationship

Was her desired end.

Despite these positive vibes,

The Junta kept tight control.

Visa renewals were impossible,

Even with a kickback toll.

I nixed living in Laos.

It had more than one con.

Its only action place:

The dirty border town of Vientiane.

Kunming – The capital city of Yunnan Province in the southwest of China. Kunming is nicknamed the Spring City due to its year-round mild weather. In the early 1990's, due to its sparse population and wide streets, Kunming was a pleasant place to ride a bicycle.

Jinghong – The main city in the southern most prefecture in Yunnan Province. Although Jinghong is three hours from the border, it is the place where deals are brokered. Minority ethnic groups account for two thirds of the population. Several of these minorities, such as the Lahu, are cousins to the same groups in Northern Thailand.

When visiting some of the Buddhist temples in this remote region of communist China, it was interesting to note they had pictures of the King of Thailand on their walls.

Also, Laos limited visas

To little more than a week.

No renewals. Period.

No matter what you seek

I flew to Kunming a few times,

And then headed south.

But, the China - Burma border

Was a steel-locked mouth.

I bummed around Jinghong

For several nights.

The dingy backroom bars

Offered curious sights.

Jesus Christ Superstar Monks

In those places,
Playing darts and shooting pool,

Young Buddhist monks

Seemed to be the rule.

They smoked weed, teased bar girls,
And downed straight booze.

They also sported sunglasses

And were handy with pool cues.

All the monks were trim,

Rugged, confidant, and cool.

They seemed to be grads

Of the Jesus Christ Superstar School.

Mule – Someone who is used by a drug smuggling gang to physically move the drugs between countries by carrying them on their person. In this case, the mules had a primary, full time job as drug smugglers. In other cases, in Southeast Asia, criminal gangs hire naive western backpackers to be their one-time mules.

The backpackers get paid in cash or plane tickets; enjoy the money; and the thrill factor they feel from being a one-time smuggler. Unfortunately, Bangkok's Bang Kwang prison is full of young backpackers who wanted to add a little more adventure to their travel itinerary. Moral: It is truly unwise to compete in activities where the military and police hold major stakes.

Twenty Kilos – Twenty kilograms. Twenty kilos is equal to 44 pounds.

H – One of the many nicknames for heroin.

Later, I learned their real job –

Drug smuggling mules.

Border guards give monks a free pass
without any rules.

These Superstars moved easily

From country to country,

With robes hiding 20 kilos of H,

That no one could see.

They traveled freely

Between Jinghong and Chiang Mai

With no other words

Than "Bless you," and "Goodbye."

Party Boss – Often, the Party Boss is the local Secretary of the Communist Party. He insures the Party has a steady revenue stream and gets its fair share of the various activities in town. More often, he also makes sure that he gets his very large personal piece of the action.

Often, small town Party Bosses are neither intelligent nor charismatic. They have moved up the ladder of success and obtained their positions through family connections or *Guanxi*. If you plan to spend any time in China you must learn the term, *Guanxi*. *Guanxi* is best described as political connections or doing a favor to a higher up in order to get him or her to do something for you.

A hotel tour guide advised,

"Best you meet the Party Boss."

Without his blessing

I could suffer a very serious loss.

"You and I are now partners,"

He said, "Welcome to town.

1st, give me US $10,000 up front.

Never write anything down."

After going through the Triangle,

Part by part.

I concluded Chiang Mai

Was the best place to start.

Chiang Mai

I had a backup plan,

Just to reduce any doubt:

The midnight train to Bangkok,

If things turn totally south.

Chiang Mai is at
the Triangle's southern tip.

From here, the entire world

Is an easy trip.

A fort-like old town

With a moat and walls,

Known for ethnic crafts

And night bazaar stalls.

Chiang Mai Map

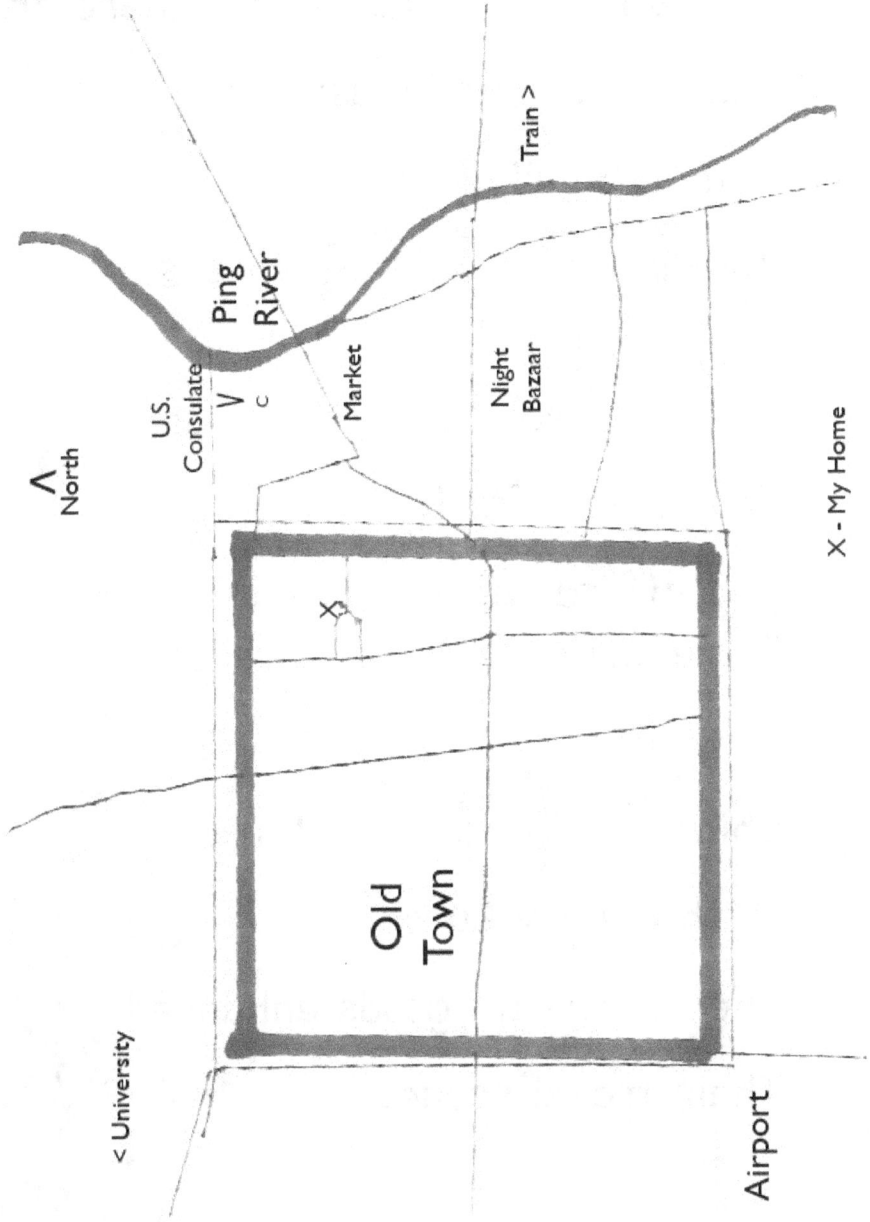

^ North

Ping River

U.S. Consolate
v
c

Market

Train >

Night Bazaar

X - My Home

Old Town

< University

Airport

X

For Bangkok's middle class, there are

Many to-dos and must-sees,

Lots of family fun

And low-cost shopping sprees.

It offers Northern Thai cuisine,

Snacks and fruits,

And affords opportunities
To renew one's Buddhist roots.

Chiang Mai's also popular

With elderly Europeans.

The handicraft goods enhanced

Their travel scenes.

While Chiang Mai is the second largest city in Thailand after Bangkok, it is still a small town. Its population is only one-fifteenth the size of Bangkok.

Many of its inhabitants are countryside farmers who have moved into the city for better paying jobs. They have large extended families whose members continually gravitate back and forth between the city and the farm.

The Old Town has a square shaped outline. Each side having a length of about one mile. For romantic charm, a moat surrounds the old town and Buddhist temples dot the landscape. There is literally a temple on every block. You know you're not in Kansas anymore.

Buddhist – Thailand is a Buddhist country around 94% of the population is Buddhist

Throw in European restaurants with
Excellent German and French chefs.

The town scores high.
It's enjoyable and picturesque.

There are Buddhist temples

Wherever you face.

Tour books claim there are 300

In this small place.

Visitors enjoy

The town's easygoing feel,

Unaware of its ugly underbelly

That's very, very real.

French Chefs & Buddhist Temples

Twenty-somethings come here

For unique thrills:

Rafting, elephant rides,

And trekking in the hills.

The hostels are cheap

And very laid back.

"Relax. Enjoy. And guys, Um, maybe

You wanna buy some smack?"

Here's where the Triangle's

Details unfold,

And why people say

It's made of gold.

Wanna Buy Some Smack?

It's the poppy flowers
Growing just north of here.
They convert to heroin,
98+% pure.

As a young jarhead,
Stories were told,
Of flower-laced fields
Magically turned into gold.

G.I.'s tasted this forbidden fruit
During the Vietnam War.
It brought cheap nights of fun
And was easy to score.

Smack – Nickname for heroin.

Traffic - Unfortunately, in recent years, due to the increased number of automobiles, pickup trucks and motorbikes, Chiang Mai has lost much of its charm and has gained a few traffic jams. This has happened in many small towns in Asia. The main streets, that in the past served only the local townsfolk, have now become major thoroughfares for cross-country trucks and buses.

98+% pure – As the poppy flowers of the Golden Triangle are the source, the heroin available in the Triangle towns is as good as it gets.

Jarhead – Nickname for a US Marine.

G.I. – Nickname for US soldier.

During Nam, the draftees

Were 18-year-old guys.

Farm kids from Iowa and Nebraska

Learned to make buys.

Our young troopers were quick

To learn first hand

The joys and pleasures

Of exotic Thailand.

The Thai beachfront
was the fun place for R&R.

Pattaya Welcomes You!

Party time in every bar.

Pattaya

Fun City

Thai drugs, booze, and gals

Known for their smile.

They made this crazy Vietnam War

Seem almost worthwhile.

The '60's Hippy culture turned opium
into a world-class thing

As for processing poppy flowers,
North Thailand was the king.

Whether Palermo Mafioso

Or Hong Kong Triad Tong

For pure white powder,

You flew to CNX before very long.

R&R - *Rest and Recuperation*, or *Rest and Recreation*. (Your choice.)

Pattaya - A southern beach town two hours from Bangkok. Pattaya has a 24/7 party atmosphere and the reputation of being the Sodom and Gomorrah of Thailand. Pattaya got this reputation during the Vietnam War, when the American Forces started using the town for R&R.

During Nam, Pattaya was the fun place to go. The door-to-door trip from Tan Son Nhat (the Saigon airport) to a beachfront hotel in Pattaya took four hours. A G.I. fighting in the Nam jungles, could get a one-week leave pass at noon, and by evening be sitting in a Pattaya beachfront beer bar with a pretty Thai gal saying, "What would you like me to do for you?"

Pattaya is not located in the Golden Triangle. Rather, it's a twelve-hour drive from Chiang Mai. But, because of its *Anytime is Party Time* atmosphere, the two towns have close opium trade links.

Back in the day,

Chiang Mai was a Wild West town

Before walking outside,

You took a quick look around.

Do you have plans for tonight?

Do you want to come home alive?

Then follow best practice –

Pack a loaded .45

Then our Saigon embassy was overrun

In late April '75.

Our last choppers pulled out,

Our Marines lucky to be alive.

Wild West Atmosphere & Loaded .45's

With the war ended, the US

Could have exited this opium tale,

Except for a Chinese-Shan rebel
leader just released from jail.

He was a ruthless jungle killer.

Khun Sa was his name.

War Lord Extraordinaire

Was the goal of his game.

A Russian doctor hostage swap,

Freed him in Sept '74.

He returned to the poppy fields

Eagerly planning his next score.

War Lord

Extraordinaire

Opium gave Khun Sa the power
And cash he sought.
His one goal - Controlling the heroin;

whether grown, sold or bought.

He knew the trails and hill tribes,
From Yunnan to Chiang Mai.
His troops ruled the jungles.
Small town mayors? Easy to buy.

Want some insights
Into Khun Sa's shtick?
Check out Denzel's
American Gangster flick.

Golden Triangle Map

CHINA

Lijiang
Kunming

Mae Kong

Yunnan

Jinghong

BURMA
(MYANMAR)

Naypyitaw

LAOS

Chiang Mai

HWY1

HWY 118

My Baan

Vientiane

THAILAND

Rangoon
(Yangon)

Bangkok
Pattaya

VIETNAM

The Triangle's military and police
quickly got the news.

Money or Death? Khun Sa made deals
you couldn't refuse.

One tale concerned a village chief

Who committed a big No-No.

He sold his town's opium harvest

To Khun Sa's long-time foe.

When Khun Sa arrived,

His army lined up every family in town.

With bullets to the heads, each man,

woman, and child was mowed down.

Shtick – Area of interest or area of activity.

Denzel – The Hollywood film star, Denzel Washington.

American Gangster – A Hollywood film released in 2007 that starred Denzel Washington and Russell Crowe. In the film, Khun Sa was portrayed by the British actor, Ric Young. The film showed Khun Sa's direct connection to the New York City drug trade.

Khun Sa moved his HQ

From Burma to Northern Thailand.

Chiang Mai offered international
logistics to market his brand.

Khun Sa's brother-in-law

Was a high-up in the police.

With payoffs to army generals,

He had security and peace.

During Nam, the US sought partners

To join our quest

For highland fighting in Nam,

The Montagnards were the best.

Nam – Nickname for Vietnam. This nickname was commonly used by G.I.s during the Vietnam War.

Montagnards – A hill tribe in Southeast Asia. The name comes from when the French had control over Vietnam. In French, the word means *Mountain People*. The Montagnards have been put down and persecuted by the Vietnamese for centuries. When the Americans joined the Vietnam War, the Montagnards were viewed as a likely ally. They proved to be an excellent choice. They knew the terrain and they were literally at home living under harsh conditions in the mountains.

Degars – Common French nickname for Montagnards.

Yards – Common American nickname for Montagnards.

They teamed with
US Special Forces early in the war.

Call 'em Yards or Degars,
they rank high in Green Beret lore.

The Vietnamese mocked the Yards
As dumb mountain folks,

Someone to cheat or ridicule
And make the butt of jokes.

But these rugged mountain men
Were brave, fierce and strong

For jungle fighting partners,
The Berets could not go wrong.

Green Berets – The popular name of the American Army Special Forces that was established in 1952. The Special Forces wore Green Berets unofficially and sometimes controversially for several years, until 1961, when President Kennedy authorized the Green Beret to be the official headgear of the Special Forces. Kennedy held the Special Forces in high regard and wanted them to stand out from other military units.

The Green Berets first came to Nam in June 1957 with the responsibility of training indigenous teams to combat the North Vietnamese and the Vietcong. They found the Montagnards to be willing and able warriors who were quite skilled at guerilla warfare. The two organizations formed a close bond that continued beyond the war years.

They'd been downtrodden in Nam
For hundreds of years;

But in their jungle home,
They were bold without fears.

Victims of bigotry gave them

An inborn hatred for the VC;

They'd gladly slit Charlie's throat
Before you count to three.

During peacetime, the Yards were

A typical hill tribe lot,

Self-sufficient subsistence farmers,
With just enough to fill their pot.

Viet Cong – Officially known as the National Liberation Front, the Viet Cong aligned with the North Vietnamese in their fight against the South Vietnamese army and the Americans. Often, the Viet Cong operated as small units of guerilla fighters. Confrontations between Montagnards and the Viet Cong were not uncommon.

The Viet Cong played a major role in the 1968 *Tet Offensive*, one of the major military campaigns in the Vietnam War. During the Tet Offensive, the Viet Cong and North Vietnamese army attacked more than 100 towns and major cities in South Vietnam. The Tet Offensive proved to the world that the opposition to the South Vietnamese government was much greater than the US military leaders had believed.

Where'd they get cash? The poppy
Flowers flourishing in the hills;

The white powder from those poppies
Easily paid the bills.

But, you can't process a harvest,
When fighting in a war.

Meeting their dilemma, Uncle Sam said,
"I'll handle that choir".

The CIA's solution was just two
Countries away.

Khun Sa would handle the process
And with US dollars, gladly pay.

Poppies - Virtually all the hill tribes in Southeast Asia grow opium poppies as a source of revenue. The Montagnards are no exception. Southeast Asia's climate is ideal for growing poppies. The flowers grow in the wild. Their short growing cycle makes them an ideal, profitable cash crop.

CIA – The US Central Intelligence Agency. The CIA gathers foreign intelligence, while the FBI gathers domestic intelligence. The CIA is often criticized for its involvement in sinister, sleazy and questionable activities.

DEA – The US Drug Enforcement Agency.

LZ – The Landing Zone for helicopters.

Chopper – A nickname for a helicopter.

Chinook - A large helicopter that can carry up to three dozen troops and fly more than 180 miles per hour. If there are less than a half dozen troops aboard, the remaining space can be used for cargo.

The problem? Logistics.
Moving the poppies 700 miles.

Nodding at the LZ,
The CIA guy was all smiles --

"1st Cav, I wanna borrow a chopper.
No questions asked.

Give me a Chinook.
They're big and they're fast."

"Get me a fresh crew,
That's all set, and ready to fly.

Their bonus: a night of R'n'R
In old Chiang Mai."

1st Cav - The 1st Cavalry Division or 1st Air Cavalry Division became a major air assault unit during the Vietnam War. The 1st was the first unit to use helicopters on a large scale for virtually every aspect of military involvement. The 1st Cav's insignia. A black horse's head on a yellow shield.

"Tell 'em, in Asia,
Chiang Mai gals are Number One.

It'll be party time, big time
When the job is done."

"My guy will meet your team
When they touch ground.

Within a day or two,
Your guys 'll be homeward bound."

"Khun Sa's the name of the Dude
We're dealin' with.

My guy has set it all up,
No worry. There won't be no shit."

Chiang Mai Gals – The young women of Chiang Mai are considered to be some of the most beautiful women in Thailand. Coupling this with their small town, country girl charm, many Asian men consider Chiang Mai girls to be ideal wives. Part of their attractiveness is due to their very fair complexions. In Asia, light skin is often viewed as being a very desirable beauty feature. The fair complexions can be traced to the influx of light skinned Burmese people during prior centuries.

Although the author did considerable research on this subject, during his thirty years of living and traveling in Asia, he did not reach any definitive conclusions as to whether Chiang Mai girls are the loveliest in Asia. He feels he would need to do much more research before reaching any clear and definitive conclusions.

"It'll be US cash, up front,
When we make the deal.

My guy'll do the countin'
And make sure the bills are real."

"Khun Sa wants the USA
To be his friend.

The whole thing should go smooth
From beginning to end."

"But, keep your backup
fully loaded . . . just in case.

After all, you'll be deep inside
Khun Sa's jungle base."

Keep your Backup fully loaded

The first shipment went well.
Then, a couple after that.

Everyone was happy.
A Win-Win. Tit for Tat.

Another one of our CIA's
Untold secret wars.

This time, our spooks aided the Yards
In making some big-time scores.

If you can't believe Uncle
Ran a long-term drug deal.

All I can say is, "Come on,
Grow up and get real."

Religion is the opiate of the Masses
- Karl Marx

Opium is the religion of the mountains
- PeriRac

And also,
Please tell me why,

Black Horse Chinooks were seen
Frequenting the Chiang Mai Sky.

The Company does interesting things
To keep bad guys at bay.

Is it red, white and blue?
Or 51 shades of gray.

In April '75, Nam abruptly ended;
The USA did an about-face;

Then, USA police chiefs screamed,
"Heroin's flooding the place."

Uncle or Uncle Sam – Nickname for the USA.

Spook – A nickname for a CIA operative.

The Company - A nickname for the CIA.

Manuel Noriega – Panama's dictator from 1983 until 1989. From the 1950's thru the 1980's, Noriega was a valued CIA drug informant and also a major drug trafficker. The CIA turned a blind eye to this.

In late 1989, Noriega pushed the envelope too far and ticked off Uncle Sam to the max. Shortly thereafter, on December 20, 1989, the USA invaded Panama. Noriega went on the run and took sanctuary in the Vatican Embassy. The USA chose to employ psychological warfare and good old fashion blaring Rock'N'Roll music. I don't know if Noriega was into rock music in his teens, but by his late 50's he could no longer suffer it. On January 3, 1990, Noriega gave up. Since then, Noriega has been held in prison.

Khun Sa, a helpful friend?
Real fast, that story grew old.

Similar to Panama's Noriega,
We threw Khun Sa out in the cold.

First, cool silence; then Uncle Sam
Reared his ugly head.

Uncle announced, "We want Khun Sa
D-E-A-D dead.

It didn't sink in with Khun Sa
Right away.

First, he's a rejected suitor;
Now, he's the USA's hunted prey.

We Want
Khun Sa
D - E - A - D
Dead

Khun Sa wanted to believe
He was still part of team USA.

"Can't we just go back
To the old way?"

He sent his guys to check.
"Is it true or not?"

They feared to report back.
Bad news Messengers often get shot.

The USA then repeated:
"Khun Sa's gotta go down."

When it finally sunk in,
He took it with more than a frown.

Shoot the Messenger

In Bangkok, the capital, the diplomats
All agreed and played nice.

But, up in Chiang Mai,
Everything came with a price.

Chiang Mai, with its tourists, banks
And bars, was a commercial core.

It was also a financial hub;
A great place to make deals and score.

The USA Consulate in Chiang Mai
Had an office for the CIA.

Now, due to opium trade,
It set up another, for the DEA.

American Consulate

The USA needed a no-nonsense guy
To combat the wrong.

They brought in Mike Powers:
Intelligent, tough, and strong.

Just by doing his job, Mike
immediately caused flack.

Khun Sa decided, "Now it's my turn
to push back."

Mike had a wife, Joyce, and
Two toddlers. A true family man.

Khun Sa included this factor
Into his evil revenge plan.

It seems it is not uncommon for our US DEA offices and CIA offices to follow paths that lead to results that are contrary, if not contradictory. Sometimes, one agency chooses to look the other way, when one of its operatives or informants is doing things that are normally considered illegal, such as dealing drugs. Meanwhile, the other agency is trying to halt this activity.

Consequently, we have had various bed partners at various times, who at other times, we choose to lock up. Khun Sa, Noriega, the Montagnards, and the whole Iran-Contra Affair are some examples. One other example in Northern Thailand is the Chinese village of Mae Salong, now known as Santikhiri, near the Burmese border. While the village is remote, it is accessible by automobile. Elements of the KMT, the Chinese nationalist army that was fighting Mao's communist forces, fled there when Mao took power in 1949. That story must wait for another day and another pen.

Mike's family went to the market,
One day just around noon,

They were savagely attacked
By a gun-wielding goon.

The hit man was told he had back-up,
And a getaway car.

But in truth, Khun Sa didn't want
This goon to go anywhere far.

We all know, dead goons
Tell no tales.

In addition, bosses don't want them
To leave any trails.

In general, criminals in Thailand are neither confrontational nor aggressive. Normally, behind the back acts of thievery are much more common than crimes of face-to-face robbery. During my time, Thailand and my many visits, I only witnessed a few physical attacks on other persons.

Thailand is known as the Land of Smiles. This is more than just tourist brochure propaganda. It is true. People will always smile at you, no matter what the occasion. Even when someone hates you, he or she will still smile at you.

Just remember, when you go to a Thai bar and a girl smiles at you, it doesn't mean she thinks you are sexy. It simply means she is Thai. Nothing more.

The goon was shocked. His getaway
car sped away during the grab.

In panic, he yanked Joyce and one kid
Into a small truck's cab.

"The escape car's gone?
That not part of the plan!"

Then six police appeared.
The goon thought, "I'm a dead man."

The family maid had run to Mike's
Office to get him into the fray.

Mike hurriedly rushed. "Gotta get
Joyce and kids out of harm's way."

Chiang Mai Market Area

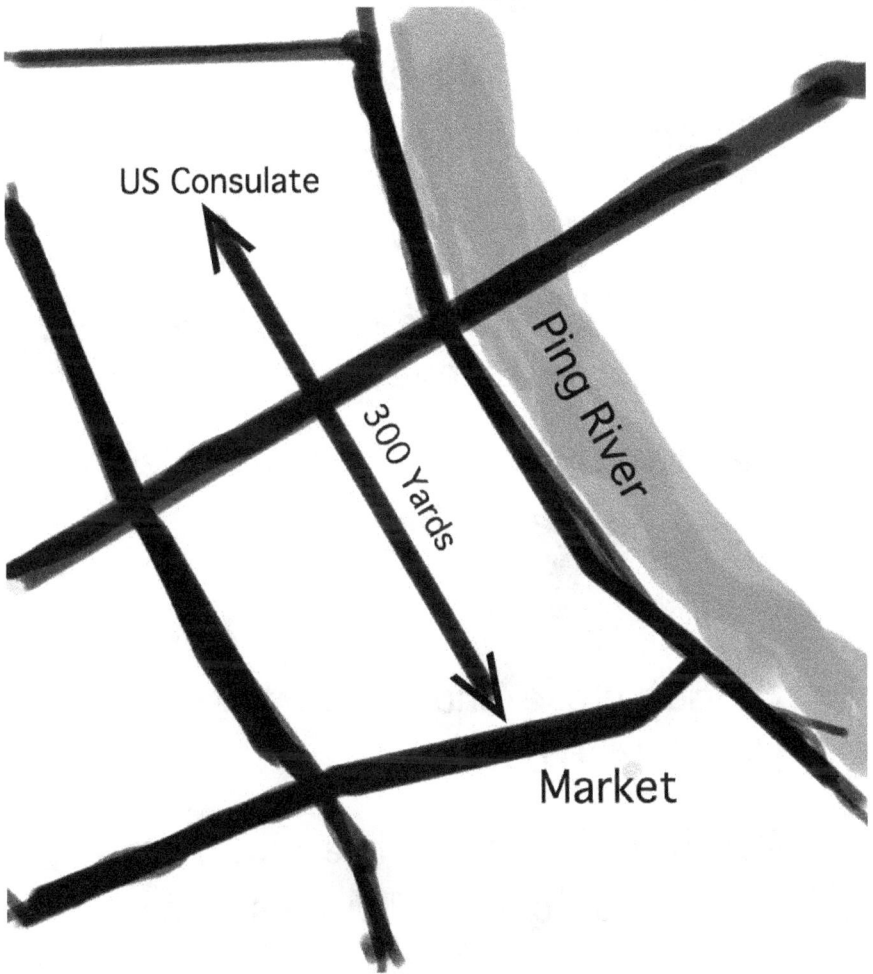

US Consulate

Ping River

300 Yards

Market

Mike stripped to his waist,
Showing no gun or knife.

His negotiation plea:
"Swap me for my son and wife."

Slowly, Mike moved closer to the goon,
Almost eye-to-eye.

He repeated, "Be Calm. Jai Yen Yen,"
Using his best Thai.

He got close enough to take
His child from his wife.

Passing his son to the maid, he
Returned to save Joyce's life.

Jai Yen Yen!
Be calm!

More police arrived
To carry out their part

The goon now knew
He'd been set up from the start.

Khun Sa owned the police,
The goon knew with dread.

The encircling cops had plans
To shoot him dead.

He pressed the gun barrel
Against Joyce's ear.

Her eyes quickly filled
With helpless fear.

Along with the cultural tradition of always maintaining a smile, another Thai trait is negotiation. If you are doing business in Thailand, always be ready for Tit for Tat, and Give and Take negotiation. This is true, even when making a small purchase from a street corner vendor. You will be more readily accepted in Thai society and be much more at ease, when you learn these Thai skills.

When Thais choose not to negotiate, that indicates something is very wrong in the situation. It may well be something you do not understand and it may be in your best interest to back out of the circumstance. The Chiang Mai gunman didn't have a chance to do this. The police had no plans to allow him to back out.

Slowly, Mike walked closer, pondering,
"What can I do?"

Through her tears, Joyce mouthed,
"Honey, I love you."

Then, a loud, Blam!
Joyce's head exploded and shattered.

The windshield turned grey-red.
Blood and brains splattered.

Silence for a moment, then Mike
Screamed with deep pain.

Next, police guns roared from all sides.
And the goon was slain.

Joyce Powers
American

Requiescat In Pace
October 1980

Requiescat In Pace – Latin: Rest in Peace.

Now Uncle was truly seething
From Bangkok to D.C.

Its next missive to Thailand –
A no-nonsense decree.

If you want USA aid
To continue to come forth?

Then take immediate action.
Clean up the North.

Bangkok sent Elite Thai Rangers
To resolve the matter.

Their singular order - Bring back
Khun Sa's head on a platter.

Thai Rangers

But this was the North,
And corruption ran deep.

Khun Sa was tipped off
Before the rangers could leap.

While the next ranger attempt
Met with limited success,

Khun Sa learned, by staying in
Thailand He'd never get any rest.

And probably, within months,
He'd be gunned down in a fight.

Khun Sa was pragmatic.
"If I wanna live, I gotta take flight."

Fight or Flight

Returning to Burma didn't mean
Khun Sa lost control.

It simply meant he had to add
More middlemen to his dole.

It also meant Burma's Junta
Could force him to play more nice.

And, naturally, the Rangoon generals
Raised their kickback price.

As for me, life in slow Chiang Mai
Made for an easy time.

With that Powers' exception,
There was zilch confrontational crime.

In addition to being totally corrupt, the Burmese Junta is also, totally paranoid and superstitious. Let me correct that. If you think everyone hates you and wants to get rid of you, and it's all true, then you are not paranoid. Correctly, then, the Junta is quite superstitious. In 2005, they feared their own citizens and several foreign elements wanted to overthrow them. What to do? They hurriedly moved the whole government some two hundred miles inland from Rangoon to a farmer's field in the middle of nowhere. This new location, called Naypyidaw, is now the country's capital. Who guided them to do this? A fortuneteller! Yes, a soothsayer who for a fee and favors told them to *Get out of Dodge*. Many civil servants were not informed about the move until 24 hours before it took place. Interestingly, all the foreign embassies chose to stay put in Rangoon and not move to the new location.

Get out of Dodge – American slang that advises people to leave town.

Chiang Mai town is truly
A compact place.

I could walk around it
At a comfortable pace.

Shortly, I found a two-story,
Three-bedroom home,

With a central location,
From which I could easily roam.

My maid oversaw things.
She had a hut out back.

From our many fruit trees,
She'd fix me a daily snack.

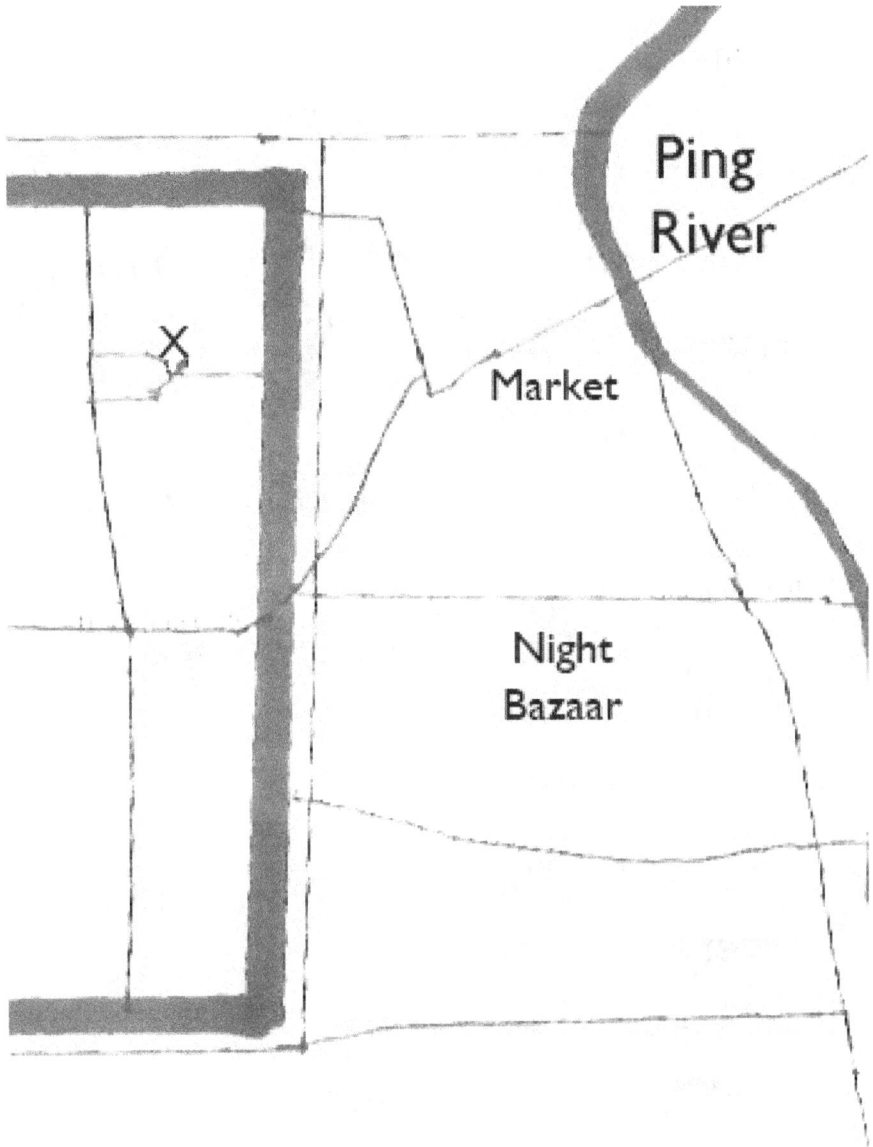

X - The location of my old home, just inside the moat at Moon Muang Soi Jet.

I befriended my landlady
And the two men in her life:

The first: a powerful local politician.
She was his Little Wife.

The second: their twenty-year-old son,
Boom. He was both shy and gay.

I noticed Daddy was greatly saddened
By his effeminate way.

The pol's other children
Were from his # 1 wife.

The son: a doctor. The daughter chose
Dad's political life.

In Thailand, a long-term mistress is known as a **Little Wife**. In many Asian countries, **Little Wives** are fairly common among businessmen and government officials. Many businessmen see a **Little Wife** as proof of success. With many poor country girls coming to the city with limited education and job skills, it is not unusual for a businessman to have one or two mistresses. The young lady doesn't have to work. She gets a free apartment, meals and spending money. If he's real busy, she only has to service him a couple times a month.

There is a whole protocol for **Little Wives**. You can take her with you to dinners and evening drinking parties with your close business associates, but you cannot take her to formal meetings with high-ranking government officials. The latter would be too insulting to **Wife # 1**.

In this case, **Wife # 2**, the **Little Wife**, was a college-educated woman and had been with the Pol (Politician) for decades.

They both held deep animosity
For Wife # 2.

Also, as they lived in Bangkok,
Our Meetings were quite few.

Alone in Chiang Mai, Boom seemed lost,
Despite his kind and gentle heart.

Coupled with shy and timid ways,
I couldn't tell if he was smart.

His folks asked me to advise him.
I tried to be his friend.

But a few lunches showed me,
we had no common grounds to blend.

Many young men in Thailand are quite reserved. They tend to be on the shy side and be a bit more gentle and sensitive when compared to western men. This can lead outsiders to believe the guys are gay. While Thailand does have its fair share of gays, you are advised not to make quick judgments. Your personal cultural experiences may be much more limited than you care to admit to yourself.

Many girls find Thai guys to be refreshingly polite when compare to their western counterparts.

His folks appreciated my efforts.
They knew I had tried.

Due to this, and other matters,
They took me on their side.

I even sat in on some stuff
Of the backroom kind.

As I didn't speak much Thai,
No one seemed to mind.

Once they tried smuggling
Two BMWs by raft.

Unfortunately, boating skills
Are not a gangland craft.

Two Beamers Gone in 60 Seconds Flat!

When navigating swift, deep rivers,
Rafts need a balanced load.

Now, the Mae Kong River is
The Beamers permanent abode.

Every three months, I'd do
A Visa Run from Chiang Mai.

The fastest and easiest choice
Was to fly.

I'd just hop a plane
Heading to China's Kunming.

With its ninety-minute flight time,
I kept it a low-key thing.

Beamer – BMW automobile.

Visa Run - Foreigners living outside their home country are commonly referred to as Expats (expatriates). Depending on many factors, Expats can be required to leave the host country at a certain frequency and for a certain amount of time. This is called a Visa Run. In my case, during my Thailand stay, I had to exit the country every 90 days to renew my visa.

Normally, I'd fly to Kunming, China; spend a few days and then return to Chiang Mai. Sometimes, for a change of scenery, I would fly to Singapore or try KL or Penang in Malaysia.

I chose to keep these Visa Runs low key. Only a couple of my friends knew when I left or when I returned. If associates asked where I'd been, I'd just say I'd been sick and resting.

KL – Nickname for Kuala Lumpur.

In the early '90's, Kunming saw
Few Yanks as a rule.

Local college kids liked to hang
With me. It made them feel cool.

I had many party invites
To discos or someone's home.

My hotel rental bicycles,
This made it easy for me to roam.

Once, I arrived just in time
For Stop Drug Trafficking Day.

Five military trucks drove around,
Showing off their display.

Actually, Kunming was home to a number of Yanks in the past. That was during World War II, when Kunming became the home of the American *Flying Tigers*.

You need to have a little backstory to know the *Flying Tigers*, whose official name was the *1st American Volunteer Group*,

In China, it is difficult to know the backstory, because for more than fifty years, the Communist government has covered up the major role American fighter pilots played in saving China's rear end.

During my visits to Kunming in the early 1990's, I was able to locate a few old timers who told me about the *big and strong* looking Americans on Kunming's streets.

The *Flying Tigers* first aerial combat mission was on December 20, 1941. They brought the fight to the Japanese, while the rest of the US military was still reeling from the shock of Pearl Harbor.

There must have been thirty plus men
Bound up on each truck's flatbed.

The message to all: mess with drugs
and you'll soon be dead.

My friend and I had rented two bikes.
"Let's see where they go."

We had to ride fast if we were going
to catch the rest of the show.

We peddled for 30 minutes.
No time to waste.

Finally, the trucks passed us
And entered a military base.

In six months, the **Flying Tigers** under General Chennault shot down 296 enemy planes and lost only 14 pilots, even though the Japanese planes were faster and much more maneuverable. The yanks used an unorthodox, high altitude **Dive and Zoom** attack plan to beat the enemy. Unfortunately, military bureaucracy, not the Japanese, did them in. They were absorbed into the 14th Air Force.

Eastern China had been under Japanese control before Pearl Harbor. The Chinese forces of Mao and Generalissimo Chiang Kai-shek were too self-absorbed in their own feud to fight the Japanese invaders. China's only supply route in the west: the Burma Road from Rangoon to Kunming.

The **Flying Tigers,** were composed of US Navy, Marine and Army pilots, under a Top Secret Executive Order signed by President F. D. Roosevelt that had them resign from the US military; then volunteer to defend the Burma Road.

The convoy had tinted-windowed
Benzes at the front and rear.

The general's faces were not visible,
Although I was near.

On that narrow road,
When the trucks entered the post,

I could see the convicts' eyes.
They all knew they were toast.

We biked past the compound.
Then climbed up a small hill.

Upon reaching the top,
A thunderous roar gave me a chill.

The *Flying Tigers* made Kunming, China their headquarters just before Pearl Harbor. Japanese pilots quickly learned they'd face extreme prejudice, if they ventured into China's western skies.

The *Flying Tigers* are perhaps best recognized by their nose art.

The *Flying Tigers* were memorialized in the book and the movie, *God is My Co-Pilot.*

The machine guns' rat-a-tat-tat
Overpowered any words I said.

When silence returned, I knew
Those poor souls were all dead.

After the machine gun fire
punctuated the air,

My friend looked at me and said,
"You gotta be fair.

America also has the death penalty.
Isn't that true?"

"Well, even in Texas, we don't do it
Quite like you."

Benz(es) – Nickname for Mercedes Benz.

China is rather secretive about many things including its executions.

There are often told stories that claim when China executes a criminal, it is done with a single bullet to the back of the outlaw's head. Later, after the execution, the government sends a bill to the family of the criminal for the cost of that one bullet. While that story is credible, I can verify, in this instance, I heard machine gun fire, not single shots to the heads. I guess in hindsight it matters little to those one hundred and fifty or more, dead drug dealers who got machine-gunned down.

In touristy Chiang Mai,
Strangers freely talked.

Informal chats were common,
Wherever I walked.

I made many casual friends
While strolling about,

I shortly knew all the cafes and bars
Inside and out.

The hill tribe peoples
I did not yet know.

The tribes had names like
Lisu, Akha, Lahu, and Meo.

Major Hill Tribes in Thailand

Lisu

Ahka

Lahu

Meo

Yao

Karen

Hmong

Palaung

I'd see their young women
Selling goods on the street.

But other than a smile and "Hello,"
We never did meet.

In Thai society, the hill tribes
Didn't quite fit,

They stayed to themselves,
And remained close knit.

My language skills being Zero,
I couldn't stop and chat.

During the first few months
I just left it at that.

For many years, the Thai government and Thai society ignored and mistreated the hill tribe peoples. Then, a few years after World War II ended, many western societies began to prosper. Around that time, air travel became more affordable and popular. The more affluent westerners got off their feet and sat down on airline seats in order to fly to Asia and other distant places.

Also, in 1949, the Thailand government formed the Tourism Authority of Thailand, known as TAT. Within a short time, TAT came to a certain realization and chose to paraphrase Mark Twain – "There's Gold in Them Thar hill tribes."

Camera totting tourists pay money to see people and things that are different. The hill tribes of Northern Thailand fit this bill. Alas, the Thai government realized by spending a few dollars on simple water lines to the villages, hundreds of tourist dollars would pour into the Thai economy. It worked.

The young women dressed
In their tribe's styles.

They negotiated with calculators
And shy, beguiling smiles.

Bargaining with them
Was sorta fun and kinda nice.

But their English was limited to,
"I give you best price."

To really know the Triangle,
You must bond with a hill tribe.

You can't do it, by short tourist treks
Or an under-table bribe.

I Give You
Best Price

I'd befriended a few hill tribe
members, who lived in Chiang Mai,

But they, after a few years in town,
Were outsiders, just as much as I.

After some time, I became friends
With two Benelux guys.

They'd been in the North for a while
And had hill tribe ties.

They were both dopers,
Sallow-eyed, more gaunt than slim.

The Dutch guy was Gerald.
The Belgian was Ahka Jim.

Benelux – The area of Europe that consists of three countries – Belgium, the Netherlands and Luxembourg. The three countries are often linked together because they are quite a bit smaller than their neighbors - France, Germany and Italy.

Doper – Someone who does drugs.

Sallow-eyed and gaunt – This can be a sign that a person is a drug addict.

Ahka – One of the hill tribes. Jim had learned the Ahka language well enough to converse fluently. He could also manage to communicate in several other Triangle languages.

Jim could meld with the tribes
Thanks to his linguistic skills.

Much of the time, he just drifted
Through the hills.

He'd mastered border crossings
In the darkness of night.

And clandestinely, he'd cross Burma
And China when in flight.

He told me, when moving China White
Got too hot,

Lijiang, with its Naxi women,
Was his go-to spot.

Ahka Jim

His occupational hazard –
Local police making a fuss,

But the pleasurable Naxi gals
Made his getaways a plus.

Whenever he drifted into town,
He kept his profile low.

What he did? Who he saw?
Local police always wanted to know.

He'd leave a coded mark on my gate,
When in town on the sly.

Usually, we'd meet in a bar
On the outskirts of Chiang Mai.

Lijiang – A city in the northwest part of China's Yunnan Province. Lijiang is a picturesque town of waterways and bridges. Its fame goes back to the ancient southern Silk Road when it was a major trade center silk embroidery center. Now, it has become a popular destination for college students on Spring Break. Unfortunately, in recent years, it has also been discovered by package tours from China's growing middle class who come in large tour buses and create Disneyland-like lines at the more scenic spots.

Naxi – The Naxi minority tend to be the majority in the Lijiang area. Naxi (modern writers call them Nakhi or Nashi), are tied to the Mosuo people and are considered to be a matriarchal society. Without getting into a sociological debate, Naxi women rule the roost, handle the money and are the main income earners. They view men, perhaps quite accurately, as irresponsible louts and drunkards who are dependable for sex and little else.

Doing drugs in the Triangle
Is not a big thing.

Smuggling 'em out?
Now, that's a different song to sing.

Too many pros
Have their vested claims.

They'll smash down any attempts
To cut into their games.

In the Triangle, police and army
Definitely held sway,

They controlled most drug trade,
Both night and day.

Police and Army Shootouts

In Thailand, it is not uncommon to hear stories about members of the Thai police getting into a shootout with member of the Thai army.

Backstory – Each of Thailand's seventy-six provinces has some sort of military presence. In those towns where there is a military installation, the young soldiers unsurprisingly frequent the bars, gambling places and house of prostitution.

Normally, the police oversee these places and get certain gratuities for the so-called protection they provide. In Army towns, the local military commander logically argues, these are my guys so I should get a piece of the action. If a suitable split is not arranged, arguments and gunfights can and do erupt.

For those Farangs,
Who were tempted to deal,

There's 10 years in Bang Kwang
To curb their zeal.

If you're new to Thailand,
There's two places you should know.

The first is, Bangkok's Khao San Road,
Where low-end backpackers go.

On Khao San, you'll find
Many types of people from afar,

You may get the feeling
You're in a Star Wars bar.

Farang – A foreigner. Farangs, normally, are foreigners from western countries. Most of the westerners visiting Thailand are Europeans or Australians, rather than Americans. Thailand is tourist friendly and the closest Asian country to Europe.

Khao San Road – An area of cheap hotels and backpacker lodgings near the old downtown area of Bangkok. Khao San Road has its own regular hourly bus from the airport. Any travel book that features **Bangkok on Ten Dollars a Day** features Khao San Road. Its cafes are casual and laidback. Backpackers feel quite free to chat with whoever is at the next table.

Bang Kwang – The notorious Bangkok prison where most foreigners end up after being arrested for smuggling or selling drugs. During the Olympics or the World Cup Games, Bang Kwang has enough foreigners from the major countries to form its own football (*soccer* for American readers) tournament.

The second is Bang Kwang prison,
A real terrible place.

Bang Kwang also houses people
Of every race.

Dreams of quick money
and being cool, you see,

Can turn a young traveler
Into a smuggling wannabe.

Gerald chose a different path:
Life in a Black Lahu baan.

He became a farmer.
He felt this had no real con.

Wannabe – Slang for someone who dreams of being someone else, such as a wannabe movie star.

Baan – In general, a baan is a small village. Hill tribe baans are often scattered in rather remote locations.

Mason Jar – A glass jar used for home canning and for preserving food. John Mason invented Mason jars in 1858. In the old days, when there were many small family farms and many people grew their own vegetables and fruits, Mason jars were quite common. They are still in use today, to a much lesser degree, with the Ball brand being the most popular ones.

.

To ease his load, he took
A 14-year-old wife.

He then settled into
A simple hill tribe style life.

Gerald grew vegetables
And helped his wife's dad.

He also grew opium.
Yeah, his cash flow wasn't bad.

He'd motorcycle into town,
And sell his stuff in bars.

Small plastic bags were
Gerald's version of Mason Jars.

Gerald
The Farmer

Different cultures moralize
On what is right and wrong.

Some pray to rain gods.
Some sing a hymnal song.

Each has unique traditions
And centuries-old ways

Their people have passed these down
Since olden days.

If you're unfamiliar
With the Lahu tribal scene,

Many Lahu gals wed
When they turn fourteen.

A 14 Year old Wife

They marry Lahu boys,
Who move in with her clan,

The boy joins her family
And works for her old man.

This arrangement goes on
For a year or two.

Drug addiction causes
Most marriages to fall through.

When they break up,
She looks to marry again.

Her dad is philosophical,
"WTF. A new hired hand."

Joint United Nations and World Health Organization study.

A joint United Nations and World Health Organization study found a high level of opium addiction among the various hill tribes of Thailand. The young male addicts were found to use 3.9 grams of opium per day and had been using opium on average for approximately eight years.

From my personal experience, I believe this study is highly accurate.

WTF – What The F*ck

Hitching up with a foreigner
Is a true rarity at best.

Her dad eagerly seeks a dowry:
"How about two grand...US?"

If the marriage is short-lived,
Her dad doesn't pout.

For sure, he's already blown the cash;
On that there is no doubt.

Gerald had been married four years
When I met Na, his wife.

With their young daughter,
They lived a simple, happy life.

The Thai government seems to view hill tribe people as outsiders. Living in remote areas, the hill tribe people move freely across open jungle and forest borders. They do not use hospitals; midwives deliver babies; and, they do not attend Thai schools. There are no birth certificates nor school records. As a matter of fact, there are no records of any kind showing proof that they are residents of Thailand. Consequently, it is nearly impossible for any of them to get a Thai passport. So, this makes it virtually impossible for them to travel or migrate to Europe, Australia or the USA.

Gerald encouraged my visits,
Welcoming me with warm cheers.
Then we'd sit up half the night,
Chatting over warm beers.

My first visit, I crashed
At Na's brother's place.

I slept on the floor.
There was barely enough space.

The guy was totally zonked,
24-7, every day.

He was hardly aware of me
during my short stay.

Sleeping in the hut of a doper wasn't too bad. He left me alone and I showed him the same respect. As a matter of fact, he hardly moved. Most of the time, he sat in a cross-legged position, just looking blankly at the space in front of him. If he would have fallen over dead, I would not have been surprised.

The hut was quite small, maybe twelve foot by twelve foot. It was not a place to hang out during day light hours. At night, in total darkness, I'd enter the hut with my flashlight and find my little sleeping mat. Within minutes, I'd be asleep. I'd awaken around sunrise and leave. Occasionally, I took an afternoon nap. The few times I saw my housemate, he was in a drug stupor and seemed not to notice me.

During that visit,
I enjoyed the village scene,

Observing the locals
In their daily routine.

Pretty much, I just relaxed
And sorta just chilled out,

I shot a lot of pictures
And just wandered about.

In opium land, a new face
Gets a suspicious eye.

But as "Gerald's Best Friend,"
I was now a Made Guy.

A
Made
Guy

A Made Guy – From gangster slang. It means someone they can trust.

The more we sat around
Drinking warm beer,

The more the villagers knew
I was no one to fear.

Occasionally, trekkers
Passed through this way.

A Lahu host can earn ten bucks
For a night's stay.

Gerald told me of an incident
From a few months before,

Concerning a trekker's new boots
Left outside a hut's door.

Trekker – Normally, the trekkers were western backpackers who were hiking around through the hills and exploring the Golden Triangle on their own.

Farang - A commonly used term for a foreigner. While its origin is argued, it seems to be tied to the name the Thais used for French people when the French had a major role in Southeast Asia. Now, Farang refers to any Caucasian foreigner. The word Farang doesn't by itself connote anything negative.

It seems wherever I go I get a nickname. In Hawaii, I am called a Haole; in the city of Guangzhou in southern China, I am called a Gweilo; in Northern China, I am a Laowai, and in Japan, a Gaijin. My attitude about it: Whatever!

Baht - The baht is the basic currency of Thailand. Currently, 35 baht equal a dollar. When I lived in Chang Mai it was 40 to the dollar.

Overnight, the boots disappeared.
His host felt deep shame.

He pled to all, "It musta been
A mistake. No one's to blame.

The Farang is leaving soon.
He needs his boots back.
No need to explain.
Just return them outside my shack."

Shortly, the Farang departed,
Wearing makeshift flip-flops.

With no one coming forward,
Discussion of the matter stops.

These boots were made for walkin'

Two days later, the host, with boots
In hand, hurried to town.

He said he found them and wanted
To track the Farang down.

Claiming success, the host returned
Within a few days.

And the baan seemed to go back
To its normal ways.

Then, a week later, a healthy neighbor
Was found dead in his pad.

All covered in vomit & diarrhea.
Wolfsbane poisoning! A very nasty bad.

Wolfsbane - Also known as Monkshood or Devil's Helmet is a truly toxic flowering plant that grows in mountainous areas.

Don't let the beauty of the plant fool you. It is extremely toxic. The Chinese have used it when hunting large animals and in battle, they would put it on the tips of arrows. Wolfsbane can start affecting the body within twenty minutes after contact.

Chinese herbal medicine practitioners use Wolfsbane in exceedingly limited amounts, to relieve pain. If you use too much, you will never, ever feel pain again.

Baht Buses - Pickup trucks that are converted into shuttle bus taxies. They are very common and convenient in the Chiang Mai area. Some roam around town, others have fixed routes to nearby towns. Their cargo areas have roofs and two long wooden benches inside. Riders hop on and off whenever and wherever they wish.

To get up to the hills,
I depended on my motorbike.

My first stop, the Baht Bus station
To sort of hitchhike.

I would cut a deal with a driver,
And throw my bike on top.

Some 90 klicks up Hwy 118,
I'd signal where to stop.

Next, it's a bumpy trail ride,
For seven more klicks.

Yeah, Black Lahu baans
Are truly in the sticks.

Normally, baht buses charge low, flat fixed rates that depend upon the destination. In town, I would pay around 5 baht for a baht bus ride. Quite cheap.

By comparison, Tuk-Tuk's, the three-wheeled taxies, often try to charge Farangs from US$5 to US$10 for a one-mile ride. Tuk-Tuk's are open aired, but have roofs.

When going to the hills, I'd motorbike to the bus station and look for buses heading to Chiang Rai. I'd tell the driver where I wanted to hop off and agree to pay extra for putting my motorbike on the roof. Other riders would get off before or after me. When we neared my destination, I'd tap on the window that separated the driver's cab from the passengers. The driver would stop the bus; I'd pay him and get my bike off the roof. Then we parted. He continued to Chiang Rai and I drove five klicks on the winding mountain path to the baan.

The small huts are
Made of bamboo and wood.

They're almost satisfactory.
It's a stretch to say they're good.

The baan's forty or so huts
Seemed to be 40 shades of brown.

Some were built on stilts,
A meter above the ground.

Others were linked together
And made into one,

Normally, for a married daughter,
sometimes for a son.

The huts are small and basic, with just one or two rooms. They do not have electricity and are dark inside. They get natural sunlight by leaving the front door open.

The cooking is done inside the hut; normally in a big pot in the center of the main room. There is no chimney. The smoke turns into soot on the ceiling.

The walls of the huts are made from pieces of wood that are loosely fit and not sealed. This allows air in and out. At first, I viewed this as poor workmanship, but because the Lahu cook inside their homes. The holes allow the cooking and heating smoke to exit the hut. In general, I did not consider the huts to be healthy places to reside for more than one or two weeks at a time.

A water supply is valuable
In any remote scene.

This baan had a water line, so that
all could cook and clean.

With the baan's dusty circumstance
And hot noonday sun,

A cool, refreshing shower
Was a relief for everyone.

While traditional Lahu clothing
Is rather chaste,

At the baan's public shower,
All went nude above the waist.

Everyone Nude Above the Waist

The shower was
The village gossip spot.

There, friends talked privately,
Out of other's earshot.

Also, each Lahu baan
Has a circular corral with a gate.

It's used for traditional dancing
During every special fete.

On Lunar New Year, the gals danced
Late into the night.

They used a couple generators
To provide adequate light.

In my experiences, traditional Lahu folk dancing is perhaps best compared to American barn dancing or round dancing. Pretty much, it is mainly the young ladies who participate. However, there is a leader, with a large mouth gourd instrument who sets the beat and pipes out the music. The gals line up shoulder-to-shoulder with perhaps two to four young ladies abreast. While guys can join in, it seemed the guys just sit around getting stoned.

The music and dancing go on for hours, with the music becoming somewhat hypnotic as the evening draws on. I don't know how late, because I got tired of watching and went back to my hut and fell asleep. In the total darkness of the hills, it is easy to fall asleep, especially if you've had more than a few shots of straight SangSom rum.

A few klicks from this baan
Was a backpacker hideaway.

A Druggie Lodge where wannabe
dopers could get high every day.

There, trekkers could try smack
Or whatever they please,

Without the ugly urban experience
Of dirty backroom sleaze.

Upon returning to Chiang Mai,
I read up on Lahu cultural ways.

And made plans to return
At Lunar New Year; all fourteen days.

Klick – *Klick* is slang for kilometer. The term is commonly used in rural areas in those countries that use meters for measurement. It is commonly used in Thailand.

A Buck – One dollar.

White Lightning – A high alcohol whiskey. Every country has one. Normally, farmers using rice, wheat or sugar cane created them centuries ago. In China, it is baijiu and the popular brand is Maotai. In Thailand, the white (or brown) lightening is called whiskey, but is more closely kin to rum. Two popular brands are SangSom and Mekhong.

Ganbei – A Chinese toast meaning empty your glass, or bottoms up.

For this visit, everyone accepted me.
I was Gerald's old friend.

This made it much easier for me
To interact and blend.

Gerald got me a private hut.
I paid US 5 bucks a night.

The owner - an old widow,
Suffering financial plight.

I ate with her family. We sat in
a circle, around a big stew pot.

They had a fire underneath
To keep the soupy food hot.

While my home in Chiang Mai was quite large and had a kitchen and all the normal kitchen appliances, I ate virtually all my meals in restaurants. The restaurant meals and drinks were quite cheap; and I enjoyed roaming around town and socializing.

For exercise, I used an upscale health club and swimming pool. For entertainment, there were many restaurants and bars. Many of the bars had live music. My social life was quite active.

This made my maid's life easy. She didn't have to cook for me. She watched several Thai soap operas every day. She had a three-room hut on the property. She acted as my home's security guard and insured no one would sneak in when I was out.

There were five types of fruit trees on the premise. My maid normally prepared a bowl of fresh fruit for me after my afternoon nap.

The old widow chomped down food
With a toothless mouth.

At every meal, this alone
Tended to gross me out.

Our stew was dished up
From a central pot.

Not too sanitary. But in the hills,
That's all you got.

If someone didn't finish
Their bowl of stew,

The leftovers were thrown back
For tomorrow's brew.

One of my friends in Chiang Mai was a Red Lahu gal who was a student at Chiang Mai University. She did not wear Lahu clothing and had left her baan as a young teen. She no longer had close ties to her old lifestyle. She told me she felt somewhat like a lost soul, as she lived on the edges of the Red Lahu, Thai and Farang cultures without belonging to any of them.

Perhaps, because of this, she chose to write her term paper for English class on the fourteen days of the Red Lahu Lunar New Year Festival. On each day, certain traditions were followed and she wanted to explain this in detail in her writings. She didn't own a computer and her written English skills were marginal. She asked if she could use my computer and asked if I would review and critique her term paper.

This paper piqued my interest in the Lahu New Year celebration. Later, when Gerald suggested I spend the Lunar New Year in his baan, I said, "Why not?"

I brought lemon juice vials
To this challenging scene,

With hopes these would kill bacteria
and keep my food clean.

One night a translator
Was invited to join our evening meal.

The widow's teen daughter-in-law
Brought him, to offer me a deal.

She wanted to dump her druggie
Husband and come live with me.

With both parents dead, she was
A bargain. There was no dowry.

Throughout my whole life, I have been unskilled when it comes to learning languages other than English. I suppose, now that I am over seventy-five, I guess I never will. I have taken formal classes in six different languages and have pretty much failed miserably at all of them. I have learned to APL when needing a translator.

When traveling in other countries, I try to learn a few key phrases: "I want a beer." "How much does it cost?" And "I think you're very beautiful." I've learned these few short phrases can take you very far.

Another travel tip: Always APL (Ask a Pretty Lady). When you need information, pull out the map. (Always carry a map, even when one's not needed. You want to look like a lost tourist.) Look for a nicely dressed gal who appears college educated. (All college students learn some English.) On a city street corner, a gal is more likely to help a lost tourist, than talk to a strange guy who appears to be trying to hustle her.

I thought, "Gal, don't talk that way
In front of your husband's clan.

You're gonna make him lose face
And be a lesser man."

Any way you look at it, I thought,
This gal just ain't cool.

She surely never learned the basics
In Mrs. Potter's etiquette school.

I told her
She seemed quite lovely and nice.

But for me,
Marriage, just wasn't in the dice.

While I lack language skills, I can eat and drink just about anything and everything. This ability has allowed me entry to many situations and acceptance in many cultures.

During my travels in remotes spots, I don't wince when my host serves dog, cat, rat, lizard or other strange delicacies.

I've eaten many types of snakes including the poisonous ones the waiter brings to the table alive. In these instances, the waiter holds the two-foot long serpent by its tail and lets it move a bit to show it still has fight.

The waiter then cuts the snake down its length with a razor and allows the blood and gallbladder to drip into the canister of white lightening. He then says "Enjoy!" as we chug-a-lug and he before preparing the rest of the snake for dinner.

Quickly I invented
A Chiang Mai girlfriend/wife.

Then I explained
How I traveled most of my life.

Later, I wondered, "My hut?
Am I renting the couple's old shack?"

"Maybe, he took off,
And isn't coming back."

Whatever. I figured it best
To stay away from this young lass.

If she'd make another offer,
I'd be curt. "No thanks. I pass."

This dinning ability has allowed me to meld with the locals in many places. In Guangzhou, where I lived for ten years, the dining guideline is, "If it has four legs and it's not the table, you eat it." I fit in well.

This ability has gained me an invite to a dinner and sleepover at Kazak horseman's family yurt in the Xinjiang Mountains. On another occasion, it took me on an oxcart ride to a home-cooked meal at a Hmong village outside Kunming. One secret: In remote places always carry a small plastic squeeze bottle of ReaLemon concentrate. It kills bacteria quickly.

During our most recent visit, a dozen Chinese Electronic Surveillance Police (old friends) hosted my wife and I in a small-town hotel. After too much *Ganbei* toasting, the Chinese government kindly comped our hotel bill. Another travel secret: I claim the only alcohol my religion allows is beer. By saying this, I avoid toasting with the more potent baijiu.

Gerald and I were chatting
On the third day.

His wife came up shyly,
With something to say.

She smiled and looked into my eyes
With excited, innocent glee.
"Can you, er, will you,
Take a shower with me?"

Caught off guard, I looked at Gerald
With a shocked fluster.

Then I quickly stammered,
"Gerald, I've never touched her."

will you
take a shower
with me?

He laughed at my embarrassment,
"No need to fear.

She wants you to live in the baan,
And feel welcome here."

Then she led me to the shower.
We both stripped to our waists.

I was shy to look at her. She, giggling,
Splashed water in my face.

Then, four of her friends ran up,
stripped down, and joined the fun.

They all liked the splash game.
It was five against one.

Five against One

The girls were emboldened.
I was Gerald's best friend and guest.

Na had Gerald's blessing. They,
As her friends, could join in the jest.

The next day, Na and her water sprite
Posse knocked at my door.

I hurried to consult Gerald,
"Again? And how many times more?"

His wife had told him, one or two gals
Had a shine for me.

And "Their dads are well aware you
can pay a high dowry fee."

One thing to learns about Southeast Asia, many relationships are related to money. Often, this is due to the income disparity. Why are the young ladies from the countryside attracted to traveling western guys? Trust me, in the vast majority of instances, it's about money. We western guys want to believe we are so cool and debonair. Maybe, we are, to a point, but then, the money factor kicks in and carries the ball over the goal line.

One Thai wife in Munich told me her story. When she was fifteen she left her village to look for a job in Pattaya. She knew her former neighbor was working as a waitress in a restaurant. She hoped her friend could help her find a job. When she arrived, she found her friend was a barmaid in a side street strip joint. Her friend was talking with a customer. She said she was leaving with the customer for an **all-nighter** and would not be back until 10:00 the next morning.

"Gerald, you know I don't want
Any kind of wife.

And a teenage Lahu gal
Won't fit in with my rambling life."

Gerald laughingly smiled and suggested
I just play along.

"Otherwise you'll offend their families.
Just don't do any wrong."

He gave me more advice to maneuver
This slippery ditch.

"Just look, but Don't Touch,
If you don't want to hitch."

Her friend and the tourist left. My friend was alone, with just a few bucks in her purse. While contemplating what to do, an Aussie sat down and offered to buy her a drink. As she had not eaten, he also bought her lunch. They talked. He took her to his room and they had sex. It was her first time. They stay together another night and he gave her US $20. She couldn't believe a man could love her that much. She was totally in love. Then, after breakfast, he told her she was nice, but he was in town for only a week and wanted to try one or two more gals before returning to Sydney.

Dumbfounded, shocked and confused, she returned to the bar. Her old girlfriend introduced her to the Mama-San who offered her a job. That night she became one more Pattaya bargirl, pulling **short-timers** and/or **all-nighters**. Six months later, a German guy showed up and offered to marry her. Now, she's a hausfrau, a housewife, in Munich. She's not really happy, but it's better than being a Pattaya bargirl.

He promised, after a few days,
He'd talk with his wife.

"In the meantime, Enjoy!
There are worse things in life."

So, Na called upon her husband's
"Best friend" several times each day.

She brought along her teenage posse,
To smile, shower, and play.

It was fun, but one night, I was
awoken by footsteps under my shack.

My half-awake thought,
"There's a gang. I'm under attack."

In the bars of Bangkok, Pattaya, Phuket and Chiang Mai it is pretty much the same. If the barmaid chooses to go with a customer, the customer must pay a bar fine to the Mama-Sa. Back then, the bar fine was US $5.00. The bar gets its money up front. After that, what happens and the amount of money paid are negotiation points between the customer and barmaid

Usually, the first factor is how long the gal will stay with the guy. An *all-nighter* means she'll stay until breakfast. A *short-timer* means she'll stay around two hours or just long enough to earn her pay.

In Bangkok, if the guy asks her to stay for a few nights, they must decide upon what to do during the daytime. The girl says she has seen all the tourist sights, but she has an idea. "Let's go to the new shopping center! I'll show you the jewelry and fashion departments, and you can show me just how much you love me."

Stilt legs held my hut up,
A meter above the ground.

Were there three or four guys
Below me, slowly moving around?

Was it a jealous lover,
Who wanted to see me die?

Had he brought some friends
To ensure my permanent goodbye?

Also, in this hilly region,
Drug smuggler groups held sway.

Had I overstayed my welcome?
Was I was getting in their way?

When you walk through the shopping malls of Bangkok, don't be surprised to see attractive young Thai gals dressed in cocktail dresses being followed by unshaven Farangs who are dressed in T-shirts, beach shorts and flip flops.

If you are a male Farang and are arriving in Bangkok for the first time, there is one thing you should know. If you want to date nice Thai women, you must always dress nice. Wear long pants and a clean shirt with a collar. If you look like a beach tourist, the Thais you pass on the street will presume the gal you are with is a bargirl. No girl wants her neighbors to think she works in a Thai tourist bar.

They'd boldly killed a DEA agent's wife
In the center of town.

In these remote hills,
It'd be easy to take me down.

I could be knifed or speared from
below While lying on my mat.

If some thrusts came upward,
I'd be dead in seconds flat.

Many thoughts bounced in my brain.
I was now fully awake.

I knew I had just a few moments,
If I were to make my break

I figured my best chance for survival
Was to stand and fight.

I prepared for a final confrontation
On that black starless night.

My only weapon
Was a simple flashlight.

I decided not to turn it on
Until I jumped into the fight.

I moved quickly, and leaped
From the door to the ground.

Doing a full 360, I surveyed
Everything as I spun around.

A
Fight
til
Death?

What I saw, caught me by surprise
And made me freeze.

Confused and bewildered,
I fell to my knees.

It took a few moments
To focus my eyes.

And see there were no killers
Nor any kind of bad guys.

My flashlight brightened the ground
Under my hut.
It showed a scene that was all butt
and gut.

When the sun goes down in the Golden Triangle, it is totally dark. The few campfires go out a few hours after sunset. After that, total darkness. Total darkness for miles and miles and miles in all directions. Only when there is a full moon is there any visibility.

It is easy to understand how past generations have had tales of ghosts and other world creatures. Lying on the floor of a hut, in total darkness, it is easy to get spooked; especially if there is any kind of wind.

Rather than crazed killers,
There were five large pigs

Chomping and nibbling
On weeds and twigs.

I felt rather embarrassed
as I chuckled at my plight

But was truly quite relieved
I didn't have to fight.

I went back to sleep knowing
I wasn't going to die.

In the morn, I decided, "Maybe,
it's time to return to Chiang Mai."

.

Piper and Black Lahu dancers.

Lunar New Year had ended, so
I headed to Chiang Mai town.

Due to my loss of appetite, my
waistline had slimmed down.

While I never chose a Lahu bride
Or even a live-in queen,

Thanks to my frequent showers,
I Stayed very, very clean.

I wondered, "For Lahu gals,
Do looks or money matter?"

After glancing in my mirror,
I conceded, alas, it was the latter.

In Chiang Mai, I had a rather active social life. I had taken early retirement. I retired at age 51, in Munich, Germany. When I rented my home in Chiang Mai, I was 52.

I had three Thai lady friends whom I saw at least once a week. All three owned their own automobiles, so economically, they were several cuts above the average Chiang Mai gal. Two of the ladies had university degrees.

The first was simply a good friend. We were not involved romantically. She was an accountant in her mid-twenties. I could depend upon her to pick me up at the airport when I arrived and see me off when I departed on one of my many trips. She also helped me when I needed a Thai perspective or something official, such as a driver's license. I saw her, maybe once a week. She wanted to learn about the west; I wanted insights into Thai mindsets.

In reflection, I don't believe I broke
Any young lady's heart.

But maybe some fathers' pocketbooks
Were sad to see me part.

Three months later, I returned to
Munich for an extended stay.
After that, it was six months of travel
and study, in the good old USA.

Because of my travels,
It was more than a year

Before I could return
to the land of Singha beer.

The second gal was a clothing designer who owned a dress shop that catered to tourists. She was in her early thirties, kind and exceedingly shy. I had trouble with her shyness, but she was a dependable friend. Sometimes, we took weekend holidays using her automobile.

The third Thai lady was a high-ranking government official, who had transferred up from Bangkok. She was 40-something; definitely, upper class; always impeccably dressed; and always looked as if she had just stepped out of a fashion magazine.

Once, we bumped into a German friend and his Thai wife. Later, my friend's wife told me, she never thought a Thai woman of that high social status would date a Farang.

I had met the government official, while buying a train ticket. We hit it off and soon were dating several times a week. Our dates often started at a health club or swimming pool, right after work.

First, one night in Bangkok,
then to the north I did fly

To my former hometown,
scenic old Chiang Mai.

First, I checked into a hotel
and rented a motorbike.

Then I checked out
the various bars I used to like.

In the morning, I rode out
To my former landlady's place.

Though very happy to see me,
Sadness covered her face.

Our dating routine had one peculiarity. We only dated from Monday to Thursday. Every Friday morning, she took the train to Bangkok and every Monday afternoon, she returned to Chiang Mai via train.

She had two rules. Other than those two rules, we had a very close relationship that could have gone further. Rule One concerned her personal life: "Ask me no questions and I will tell you no lies."

Rule Two was also simple. If I happened to be in Bangkok on a weekend, I should never, even think about contacting her. I could handle both these rules as this freed me up on the weekends, to do my thing; date other Thai gals; or hook up with Asian and Western tourists. As for Bangkok, no problem. I had several friends there, and if there's any place in the world to have a boy's night out, Bangkok's that place.

The only personal thing she shared: Her brother was an admiral in the Thai navy.

Her eyes were filled with tears.
She Looked aged and pale.

After her maid served us tea,
She unloaded her tale.

Her circumstances had changed
More than a lot.

Listening, I wondered, "Am I
One of the few friends she's got?"

Her husband and her son were gone.
Both were dead.

Now her life, a void, overshadowed
By constant dread.

In Thailand, virtually everyone has a nickname that their mother gave them right after birth. Three common nicknames Lek, Nit, and Noi all mean "small" or "tiny." Pui means, "chubby" or "plump." It is a bit comical to call a ninety-pound, thirty-year-old woman, Plump. Also, Thai women in general are quite comfortable going through life with "Chubby" as their nickname.

One of the realities of Thailand: Thai family names are unbelievably long. They normally have a minimum of twelve letters. I really appreciated the fact that they use nicknames. The down side, many gals have the same nickname. When I answered the phone and the gal says, "Hi, this is Lek." I had to try to figure out which Lek it is.

Her politician husband had died
Nine months before.

His false friends no longer came
To call at their door.

"The Strong Man of the North" was
Killed by a diseased liver.

As her story continued, her body
started to quiver.

Boom had been murdered
Three months after that.

Payback to the Little Wife?
Revenge? A belated tit for tat?

Getting around Chiang Mai can be a bit awkward if one doesn't have his own set of wheels. Initially, I walked everywhere. As I have run quite a few marathons, I never really mind walking a mile or two. However, as the daily Fahrenheit temperature in Chiang Mai is regularly in the nineties, I knew I was going to sweat a lot. Also, the main streets are always congested with traffic, noise and pollution. This makes it generally unpleasant to walk around town.

The baht buses are an economical way to hop around the city. Normally, I took my motorbike or a baht bus, when I went shopping; visited a doctor or went to other places that were not part of my daily routine.

Boom had gone bike riding,
As he did every afternoon;

He followed a twenty-klick loop
To keep his body in tune.

By dinner that evening,
Boom had failed to return.

She then drove his bike route,
Out of fear and concern.

She found his bike and backpack
Near a drainage stream.

Later, she realized how this location
fit into the scheme.

After a few months, I bought a second-hand motorbike for a few hundred dollars. This gave me greater freedom, especially in the evenings. None of my three lady friends would ride on the back of my motorbike. That was fine. We would use their cars and they would drive me around town.

Before I got the motorbike, the Tuk-Tuks would continually bother me. A Tuk-Tuk is an open cab, auto rickshaw. Tuk-Tuk drivers would continually stop me and ask, "Where you going?" Then, presuming I was a tourist, would try to grossly over charge me. US$10 for a ride that should cost US$.50. That gets old quickly, especially if it happens every time you walk down the street.

By the way, "Where you going?" is a common Thai countryside salutation. It seems to come from the small village society, when a villager saw a friend walking out of town, he was probably going somewhere he normally didn't go.

After another two days,
She discovered Boom's fate.

His body was found downstream,
Stuck in a watershed gate.

She handed me photos
Showing his head severely bashed.

He'd suffered a serious clubbing
Before his body was trashed.

The police investigation
Was quick and short:

"We found a beer can. He got drunk.
Fell in." End of report.

After buying a motorbike, the Tuk-Tuk annoyance went away. The new annoyance was the crazy, erratic drivers. But hey, life is an adventure. I was reminded of this often, especially at night, when I saw motorbike drivers crash into cars and sometimes quite literally bite the dust. Normally, I chose not to drive my motorbike at night. Too dangerous.

A second annoyance related to the fact that I had bought a second-hand motorbike. It worked fine. No problems. Most of the time, my driving distance was short – a mile or two. The annoyance was from gas station attendants and other motorbike drivers who told me as a (presumably rich) Farang, I should be driving a newer and more stylish motorbike.

I was very aware of the black market for stolen motorbikes. When I parked my old beat-up bike to have lunch, I felt very comfortable knowing no one would choose to steal it.

In the North, when the rich
And powerful have special needs,

They often call their police
connections to do their dirty deeds.

Her rental properties were seized.
She knew there's little she could do.

"Your son had misfortune.
Don't let the same happen to you."

When I rode away from her driveway,
I turned and looked back.

Her future seemed, just like
her clothing, very, very black.

My motorbike - When I left Chiang Mai, I gave the motorbike to a Hmong man who had married a Lisu woman. They lived at the foreigner cemetery on the outskirts of town. He was the caretaker.

I knew him through his daughter. She sold handicrafts in the Night Market and we had had a short relationship. He also had two preteen sons. They were a nice family and were living on very limited funds.

He was shocked and more than happy when I gave him the motorbike. I got the impression, it was the nicest gift he had ever been given. He asked me, wide eyed, a half dozen times, "You are really giving it to me?" "You mean, I don't have to pay any money?" "You really mean that?"

The next day, I headed to the baan,
Following my old routine.

There, too, upon arrival,
I encountered a disturbing scene.

Several months before,
Gerald and Na had both died of AIDS.

When dopers share needles,
They pay a price for these trades.

Also, where there was one corral,
Now stood two.

When I asked about this,
I learned something new.

It has been more than twenty years since I gave up my home in Chiang Mai and returned to Germany and the USA.

I went back to Chiang Mai a half dozen times during the first ten years. The last two times I brought my future wife with me. I wanted her to know something of my past and to see the sights of Thailand.

My three Thai lady friends:

First: My Loyal Friend – She told me she had met an American through an Internet dating website. Their conversations were getting serious and he was coming to Chiang Mai to see her and meet her family.

Since then, their relationship progressed. They married and settled in Oklahoma. Recently, I understand, they retired and moved back to her hometown in Thailand. We are now Facebook friends.

A 12-year-old Lahu girl and her
brother were out one day.

They ran into a Yank
From the Druggie Lodge down the way.

The Yank said, "Your sister looks cute.
Real, real fine.

How much do I have to pay
To make your sister mine?"

He said he'd pay top dollar,
Double the normal best.

The kid said, "US $4,000."
The Yank said, "Hell, yes!"

Second: The Dress Maker – I lost track of her. On a visit, a few years after I left Chiang Mai, I found her shop had changed hands. The new owner told me, my friend had had a family emergency. Her mother became quite ill; so, she sold her shop and moved back to her home village. The new owner told me my friend had not left a forwarding address.

Third: The Government Official – She transferred back to Bangkok around the time I left for Germany.

A year later, we did meet again, in Bangkok. It was the first time we met in Bangkok and the last time we ever met. We had a warm and pleasant dinner at an upscale Thai restaurant. At the end of the meal, we sipped brandy. Our hands reached across the table and our fingers touched. We looked into each other's eyes and said, "Goodbye."

The brother hurried home,
"Gotta talk with Dad."

The father mused, "Wow.
This offer ain't bad.

Why wait two years
And only get half that sum,

Best to maximize my income.
I ain't so dumb."

The whole village got involved
Before the deal went through.

Some voiced indignation. Others said,
"It's too good to be true."

Sawadeekap My Baan

Sawadeekap – Thai for Goodbye.

Finally, Dad got four G's and the Yank
Got sex with a twelve-year-old bride.

This split the baan. A second corral
Was built. One for each side.

My last stop, Na's family hut, before
Putting my motorbike in gear.

I bid her parents farewell,
And better fortune in the coming year.

Gerald's fair-haired hapa daughter
Had truly beautiful eyes.

Bangkok brothel procurers
Would see her as an exquisite prize.

Four G's – US $4,000.

Hapa – A mixed race person. The term is commonly used in Hawaii. Often Hapa people are quite attractive because they tend to get the best genes of both races.

The Red Lahu Girl – After I had been back in the USA for a year, I received a letter from the Red Lahu Girl. She was very depressed. She was now in her mid- twenties. She felt life was passing her by. She was sad and lonely. She wanted to know if I could find an American who would be willing to marry her. She said she just didn't fit into Thai society. With a college degree, she knew she could never live in a Lahu baan again. She felt hopeless and lonely. I wrote her a short letter saying all my friends were married and I could not offer her any suggestions. I wished her good fortune. I don't know if she ever received my letter.

I rode up a small hill,
And took a final look around.

Then, I hit the gas;
My bike was Chiang Mai bound.

From there it was CNX to BKK.
Then, back to the USA.

I sort of knew in my heart,
I'd never be back again this way.

As for Ahka Jim,
I never picked up his trail.

Hopefully, he's in a Naxi girl's arms
And not a Burmese jail.

CNX

BKK

DFW

MUN

CAN

HNL

What did my Triangle days teach me?
I'm not too sure.

But, I'll gladly share more stories,
if you're paying for the beer.

Today's Triangle? Nothing's changed;
Still a playground of the drug trade.

Through it, many top police
And army get very well paid.

As for the Yards, our Green Berets
Will always hold them high;

But, long ago, our US Government
Left them out to dry.

Will I ever return to Chiang Mai? Probably not. Maybe for a visit. It was an interesting part of my life, but it was time to move on.

After leaving Thailand, I bounced in and out of Munich and the US mainland a few times. Then, as I had lived in San Antonio for a couple years before moving to Germany, and still carried a Texas driver's license and voted in Texas, I moved back to Texas. This time, it was Waco, in order to obtain an MBA at Baylor University. Upon graduation, I was offered two positions. One offer was from a bank dealing with oil money in Almaty, Kazakhstan.

And, warlord Khun Sa? The USA
never got him, though it tried.

He shoveled enough money to the
Junta to protect his ugly hide.

Through the 1990's, he lived
In a Grand Poobah mode.

Though gradually his life of indulgent
luxury caused his power to erode.

His golf and teenage harem took on
More importance as he got older.

Gradually Khun Sa's empire was cut up
As his enemies grew bolder.

The other job offer was from China's Guangdong Province Government. The provincial government asked me to come to Guangzhou, the main trade city in South China to teach International Marketing to Chinese college students. That was in 1997. I knew China was the future, so I passed up the oil money.

The factories of Guangzhou and the adjacent Pearl River Delta produce a very large percentage of China's export consumer goods. Guangzhou's Canton Fair remains the top export fair in China.

Seeing how China has grown in the last twenty years, it seems my students learned well and now earn well. And, in retrospect, I like to think, I was a damn good teacher.

Finally, at 73, he died
of middle class ills in the Fall of 2007.

I don't know where he rots today,
But, I'll bet you ten to one,

It ain't heaven.

Sawadeekap

ABOUT THE AUTHOR

Dennis M Keating has enjoyed a peripatetic lifestyle. His international perspective and eclectic enthusiasm for life come from his forty some years in Germany; Thailand; China and Hawaii.

For the last ten years, Keating and his wife, Sandy, have been living a quiet life in Waikiki. Normally, he can be found pounding his iMac keyboard, hiking the Diamond Head trail, or strolling with his wife at sunset along the sands of Waikiki.

Keating writes on a diverse range of topics. His books draw upon his multifarious interests and personal experiences. Most of his books are nonfiction.

Keating's Facebook page:
https://www.facebook.com/TheHonoluluGuy/
He is happy to Friend you on Facebook.
In 2016, Keating released - *The Olympics: An Unauthorized Unsanctioned History*

In 2017, Keating released
Poetry for Men - Action Adventure Murder is a compilation of Keating's five poetry books.

Charlie Whitman was a Friend of Mine. The story of the Texas Tower Killer.

Ena Road. Murder and racism in Hawaii.

The Fulda Gap. A Cold War confrontation.

A Chicago Tale. A triple murder story.

Black Lahu. Opium, life and death in the Golden Triangle.

His email is **lostpuka@gmail.com**
His websites are:
GoldenSphere.com & **HonoluluGuy.com**

Keating owns all rights to the material in this book. For film rights, or for other reasons, please contact him.

www.ingramcontent.com/pod-product-compliance
Lightning Source LLC
Chambersburg PA
CBHW071337290326
41933CB00039B/1092